The Little Rock Nine

by Meredith Costain

EDUCATORS PUBLISHING SERVICE
Cambridge and Toronto

© 2008 by Educators Publishing Service, a division of School Specialty Publishing, a member of the School Specialty Family

Series Authors: Kay Kovalevs and Alison Dewsbury
Commissioning Editors: Rachel Elliott, Tom Beran, Lynn Robbins, and Laura Woollett
Text by Meredith Costain
Edited by Janet Klausner and Sheila Parsonson
Designed by Lisa Austin
Photographic research by Alice McBroom

Making Connections® developed by Educators Publishing Service, a division of School Specialty Publishing, and Pearson Education Australia, a division of Pearson Australia Group Pty Ltd.

ISBN 978 0 8388 3373 5

1 2 3 4 5 PEA 12 11 10 09 08

Printed in China.

Acknowledgments
The author and publisher would like to thank the following for permission to reproduce the copyright material in this book.

Photographs
AAP Photo, pp. 15, 25 (all), 26 (top), 27–29 (all); AAP Photo/Will Counts, p. 5; Arkansas Arts Center Foundation Collection: Gift of the Artist, Will Counts, Bloomington, Indiana. 1997.039.007, p. 7; Corbis, cover, pp. 1, 4, 6, 8, 9, 12, 13, 14 (top), 16, 17, 18, 19 (all), 26 (bottom); Getty Images, p. 14 (bottom); Getty Images/Don Cravens, p. 11; Getty Images/Cynthia Johnson, p. 24; Getty Images/Gertrude Samuels, p. 20; Getty Images/Paul Schutzer, p. 21; Library of Congress/John T. Bledsoe, p. 10; Library of Congress/Thomas J. O'Halloran, pp. 22, 23 (all); Photolibrary.com/Alamy/Elva Dorn, p. 30

Text
© NBC News, Roundtable transcript, PP. 17–19

Every effort has been made to trace and acknowledge copyright. The author and publisher welcome any information from people who believe they own copyright material in this book.

Contents

Standing Tall

Elizabeth Eckford climbed down the steps of the bus. She peered fearfully across the street. An angry mob of white people had gathered around her new school— Central High School in Little Rock, Arkansas. They were screaming and shouting. Soldiers stood guard at the school entrance. Elizabeth smoothed down the black and white dress she'd made especially for her first day. Then, head held high, she began to walk toward the mob.

Elizabeth had been warned there might be trouble. She searched the crowd for the familiar faces of the other eight African American students starting school that day. Where were they? She took a few steps toward the school.

A crowd gathers outside Central High School.

A white student enters the school grounds but National Guardsmen do not let Elizabeth Eckford pass.

The protesters moved in closer. They began to follow Elizabeth and call her names. Her knees started to shake. Clutching her books tightly, she approached a guard. She hoped that he'd guide her into the school. Instead, he made no move to let her pass.

Escaping the Mob

Elizabeth spun around. She noticed an older woman with a kind face staring at her. Elizabeth thought this woman might help. But instead, the woman spat on her.

"You're not coming into our school!" someone in the crowd yelled. "Get out of here!"

Elizabeth walks through the jeering crowd.

Once more, Elizabeth turned to the guards for help. They stared stonily ahead. She looked down the street and saw a bench at the bus stop. Maybe, if she could just reach that bench, she would be safe! Fighting back tears, she stumbled toward it. She struggled to block out the ugly words the crowd was shouting at her.

Elizabeth collapsed onto the bench. The angry crowd surrounded her once again. "Two, four, six, eight! We ain't gonna integrate!" they screamed. A white man sat down beside her and patted her shoulder. "Don't let them see you cry," he whispered. A white woman named Grace Lorch helped her onto a bus. Elizabeth's horrible experience was over—for now.

Elizabeth waits at the bus stop.

Chapter 2

Integrating the Schools

Elizabeth Eckford was one of nine black students who tried to integrate Little Rock's all-white high school in 1957. The students became known as the "Little Rock Nine." African American students and civil rights leaders had been waiting for school integration since 1954. That was when well-known civil rights lawyer Thurgood Marshall argued the famous case, Brown vs. Board of Education. The United States Supreme Court ruled that separate schools for black and white students were not equal. Therefore, segregation was not lawful.

The Supreme Court's ruling meant that all states were required to end segregation in schools. Arkansas was one of the states with segregated schools. Civil rights leaders in Little Rock felt that their city was ready to follow the Supreme Court's decision.

Thurgood Marshall (center) and other lawyers helped to win important civil rights cases.

The Little Rock Nine had met often with their adviser, Mrs. Daisy Bates. Bates was a civil rights leader. She was hopeful that these excellent students would do well at Central High School. The students knew that they were part of an important change in their state and in their nation. They expected to face trouble, but they wanted a good education. They also believed strongly in integration.

The nine teenagers had become good friends. They had been told to enter the school together on September 4, 1957. But Elizabeth's family had no telephone. She didn't know about the plan to meet before school and go together. So Elizabeth braved the mob alone.

The Little Rock Nine study together.

When Governor Orval Faubus heard about the plan to integrate Central High, he called out the Arkansas National Guard. The troops patrolled the school grounds. Their job was to make sure that only white students entered Central High that day.

The governor knew that many Arkansas voters were opposed to integration. He did not want to lose their support. But he did not say that the troops were there to stop integration. He said that he put National Guard troops on duty to "restore the peace and good order of this community."

The troops did as they were told. None of the African American students made it inside Central High School that day.

A young boy watches a protest march against desegregation.

Governor Orval Faubus talks to people in favor of segregation.

All over the country, people followed news stories about Governor Faubus and Central High School. Thurgood Marshall came to Little Rock. He said that the governor had broken the law. Governor Faubus had no right to use the National Guard to stop integration.

A team of lawyers including Marshall argued the case before a federal judge. The nine students went to court as witnesses. The judge ordered Governor Faubus to remove the National Guard troops from Central High School.

Chapter 3

A Second Try

On September 23, 1957, the Little Rock Nine arrived at Central High in two cars. City police were at the school already, trying to keep the crowd peaceful. The police quickly brought the nine teenagers into the school through a side door. Angry people outside yelled hateful words. They tried to break through the police lines and others pushed against the wooden barriers. Some people were even carried away by police officers.

A group of boys protest integration.

Demonstrators form an angry mob.

Inside the school, the black students met helpful students and teachers. But they also heard hateful comments and threats. The mob outside grew more and more violent. Some people attacked African American newspaper reporters with bricks. Finally, the police decided that the situation was too dangerous. The nine students were taken out of the school and driven home.

The President Steps In

President Dwight D. Eisenhower was following the events in Little Rock. He knew that integration was the law. The law had to be obeyed, even in places where the protests were violent.

President Eisenhower sent units of the U.S. Army's 101st Airborne Division to Little Rock and federalized the National Guard. Central High School was heavily protected. A soldier was assigned to each African American student. At last, the Little Rock Nine could go to school.

Soldiers escort African American students to and from school.

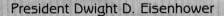

President Dwight D. Eisenhower

14

Interview with Ernest Green

Ernest Green was the oldest of the Little Rock Nine. He was the first African American student to graduate from Central High School. In 1962, a reporter asked him what he remembered most about his first day. Ernest's memories show that not all Central High students were against desegregation.

"…The most significant thing was the friendly attitude that students showed toward me the day of the rioting.

The type of thing that was going on outside, people beaten, cursed, the mob hysterics and all of this going on outside…we inside the school didn't realize the problems that were occurring and continually students were befriending us.

I remember one case in particular in my physics class. I was three weeks behind in my assignments, and a couple of fellows offered to give me notes and to help me catch up the work I had missed."

Chapter 4

Roundtable Discussion

An important meeting was held several weeks after the Little Rock Nine entered Central High School. Black students and white students met to discuss their opinions. The black students were Minnijean Brown and Ernest Green. The white students included Sammy Dean Parker, Kay Bacon, and Robin Woods.

The discussion was aired on NBC and moderated by Jorunn Ricketts. This is an edited excerpt.

White students block the main entrance of Central High.

A boy protests school integration.

SAMMY: Our Governor was trying to protect all of us when he called out the National Guard.

ERNEST: Well, I have to disagree. I know a student that's over there with us, Elizabeth. And that young lady, she walked two blocks, I guess—as you all know—and the mob was behind her. Did the troops break up the mob?

ROBIN: When Elizabeth had to walk down in front of the school, I was there and I saw that. I was very ashamed. I felt like crying because she was so brave when she did that. And we just weren't behaving ourselves—just jeering her. I think if we had any sort of decency, we wouldn't have acted that way. But I think that if everybody would just obey the Golden Rule—do unto others as you have others do unto you—that might be the solution. How would you like to have to walk down the street with everybody yelling behind you like they yelled behind Elizabeth?

Soldiers protect the African American students.

RICKETTS: Sammy, why do these children not want to go to school with Negroes?*

SAMMY: Well, I think it is mostly race mixing . . .marrying each other.

MINNIJEAN: Hold your hand up. I'm brown, you are white. What's the difference? . . . Kay, . . . Robin—do you know anything about me, or is it just that your mother has told you about Negroes?

* In the 1950s, the preferred term for African Americans was Negroes.

RICKETTS: Have you ever really made an effort to try to find out what they're like?

KAY: Not until today.

SAMMY: Not until today.

KAY: We both came down here today with our mind set on it that we weren't going to change our mind that we were fully against integration. But I know now that we're going to change our mind.

RICKETTS: What do your parents say to that?

KAY: I think I'm going to have a long talk with my parents.

Both sides express their feelings about segregation with picket signs.

The Chili-Dumping Incident

Minnijean Brown and the other eight African American students were often hassled at school. They were spat on in the halls. They were sprayed with ink. They were tripped and pushed down stairs. Sometimes they were even kicked and punched. Some of the Little Rock Nine even received death threats.

One day, Minnijean was standing in the cafeteria line. She was waiting for her lunch, and the white boy behind her was calling her names.

The white boy continued to bother Minnijean, trying to get a reaction. The server handed Minnijean a bowl of chili. By that time, Minnijean had reached her breaking point. She'd had enough. But she also knew that if she fought back, she could be kicked out of school. "Well, so what?" she thought. She just couldn't take it anymore.

Minnijean listens to a teacher.

Students get lunch in the cafeteria.

Minnijean picked up the bowl of chili and dumped it on the white boy's head. There was stunned silence. Then the African American servers behind the counter broke into applause. The white students gaped at each other. It was the first time they'd seen an African American student fight back.

Minnijean was suspended for six days. Several white students handed out cards that read, "One down, eight to go." When Minnijean returned to school, the attacks against her increased. Several white students reported that Minnijean had thrown her purse at a girl and insulted her. In February 1958, Minnijean was expelled from Central High School.

Chapter 6

Legacy of the Little Rock Nine

Eight of the Little Rock Nine completed the school year at Central High. They were not allowed to participate in sports or clubs. They were constantly bullied. They often felt terribly lonely. Yet they managed to do their schoolwork. They showed courage that inspired people everywhere.

At the end of the school year, Governor Faubus tried again to stop integration. He closed all of Little Rock's high schools for a full year.

Governor Faubus closes the schools to stop integration.

More than 3,000 students, both black and white, miss a year of school.

Some of the Little Rock Nine transferred to other schools during that year. Others studied at home or waited until the following year to complete their studies. But they all earned their diplomas.

The heroism of the Little Rock Nine has not been forgotten. In 1999, the United States Congress voted to give its highest civilian award, the Congressional Gold Medal, to the Little Rock Nine.

Sadly, Daisy Bates was not at the ceremony. She died just days before the Little Rock Nine received their medals. Bates advised the students during their battle to integrate the school. She provided them with support and guidance. Her involvement in school desegregation had a price. She was forced to close down the newspaper that she and her husband published. But she never gave up on the students. Bates gave them the strength they needed to make important changes happen.

Little Rock Nine with President Bill Clinton and Hillary Clinton at the Congressional Gold Medal award ceremony

Where Are They Now?

After their victory over school segregation, the Little Rock Nine went their separate ways. What happened to them?

Minnijean Brown Trickey

After she was expelled from Central High, Minnijean moved to New York City. She graduated from New Lincoln High School in 1959. She then went on to Southern Illinois University.

Later Minnijean and her family moved to Canada. She is a well-known advocate for civil rights. Currently she works as a teacher, writer, and speaker.

Gloria Ray Karlmark

Gloria graduated from college with a degree in chemistry and mathematics. She went on to study in Sweden. Later, she wrote and published computer magazines there. Today Gloria lives in Europe.

Ernest Green

In 1958, Ernest Green graduated from Central High School. There were 602 students at his graduation ceremony. Six hundred and one of them were white. When his name was called to receive his diploma, nobody clapped. But Ernest didn't mind. He had his diploma.

Ernest won a scholarship to Michigan State University. He worked for civil rights while he was there. He also earned two degrees in sociology. While Jimmy Carter was president, Ernest had an important job in the Department of Housing and Urban Affairs. Today he is the vice president of a company in Washington, D.C.

Ernest Green was the first African American to graduate from Central High School.

Thelma Mothershed Wair

Thelma finished her high school diploma at home. She earned her degree and became a teacher. For many years, Thelma taught home economics in St. Louis. She also worked in juvenile detention centers and taught survival skills to homeless women.

Melba Pattillo Beals

After the last day of school in 1958, Melba burned her school papers. When she was seventeen, Melba began writing for newspapers and magazines. Later she received a degree in journalism from Columbia University. Today she teaches journalism at a university.

Melba also wrote a book called *Warriors Don't Cry*. It is partly based on diaries she kept while at Central High. She is the only one of the Little Rock Nine to write a book about the experience.

Elizabeth Eckford

Elizabeth moved to St. Louis at the end of the school year. She graduated from high school there, and she studied history in college. Later, she joined the United States Army. She now works as a probation officer in Little Rock.

In 1997, Elizabeth went to a reunion in Little Rock. A woman named Hazel Bryan Massery was there. Hazel had shouted words of hate at Elizabeth forty years earlier. She apologized to Elizabeth. Elizabeth accepted her apology.

Dr. Terrence Roberts

When the schools in Little Rock closed, Terrence moved to Los Angeles. He finished high school there. In college, he studied sociology and psychology. Today, Terrence teaches at Antioch University in Los Angeles. He is also a popular speaker.

Jefferson Thomas

Jefferson graduated from Central High School in 1960. A few years later, he narrated a film about the Little Rock Nine. He said, "If Little Rock taught us nothing more, it taught us that problems can make us better. Much better." The film won an Academy Award.

Today, Jefferson lives in California. He is an accountant for the U.S. Department of Defense.

Carlotta Walls LaNier

Carlotta was the youngest of the Little Rock Nine. When Central High School opened again, Carlotta went back for her last year. She graduated in 1960.

Later Carlotta earned her degree from Colorado State College. In 1977, she founded her own real estate company. She lives in Colorado.

Little Rock's Heroes

The civil rights era in the United States brought struggle and pain. But it also brought hope and change. There were many heroes of the civil rights movement. These people took great risks and showed enormous courage to bring fairness and justice to their nation. Among these heroes were the high school students known as the Little Rock Nine.

In some ways, the Little Rock Nine were just ordinary teenagers. But they had more to worry about than what clothes to wear or whether they'd make the track team. Their courage in the face of hatred and violence inspired the nation.

Little Rock Nine statue at the Arkansas State Capitol

Glossary

advocate	someone who speaks or acts in favor of someone or something
civilian	a person who is not serving in the armed forces or the police
civil rights	basic rights of a nation's citizens
desegregation	stopping the practice of having separate schools or other public facilities for people of different races
federalize	to place something under control of the federal government
integration	the end of the separation of races
National Guard	a state's military force that can be used for emergencies within the state and is also available for use by the federal government
protester	someone who takes part in a demonstration or who complains or objects to something
segregation	the practice of separating people according to racial groups

Index